A Visit to SPAIN

by Hermione Redshaw

Minneapolis, Minnesota

Credits

All images are courtesy of Shutterstock.com, unless otherwise specified. With thanks to Getty Images, Thinkstock Photo, and iStockphoto.

Cover – leonov.o, May_Lana. 2 – ESB Professional. 4–5 – Frank Fischbach, max dallocco. 6–7 – Matej Kastelic, bodrumsurf. 8–9 –V_E, Pocholo Calapre. 10–11 – Fernando Cortes, leonov.o. 12–13 – BearFotos, Alfaguarilla. 14–15 – Kolombo Castro, Elena Eryomenko. 16–17 – TTstudio, WorldStockStudio. 18–19 –Sr_Jota, Ondrej Prosicky. 20–21 – Balate Dorin, vulcano. 22–23 –Catarina Belova, Damira.

Library of Congress Cataloging-in-Publication Data is available at www.loc.gov or upon request from the publisher.

ISBN: 979-8-88509-377-4 (hardcover)
ISBN: 979-8-88509-499-3 (paperback)
ISBN: 979-8-88509-614-0 (ebook)

For more information, write to Bearport Publishing, 5357 Penn Avenue South, Minneapolis, MN 55419.

CONTENTS

COUNTRY TO COUNTRY

A country is an area of land marked by **borders**. The people in each country have their own rules and ways of living. They may speak different languages.

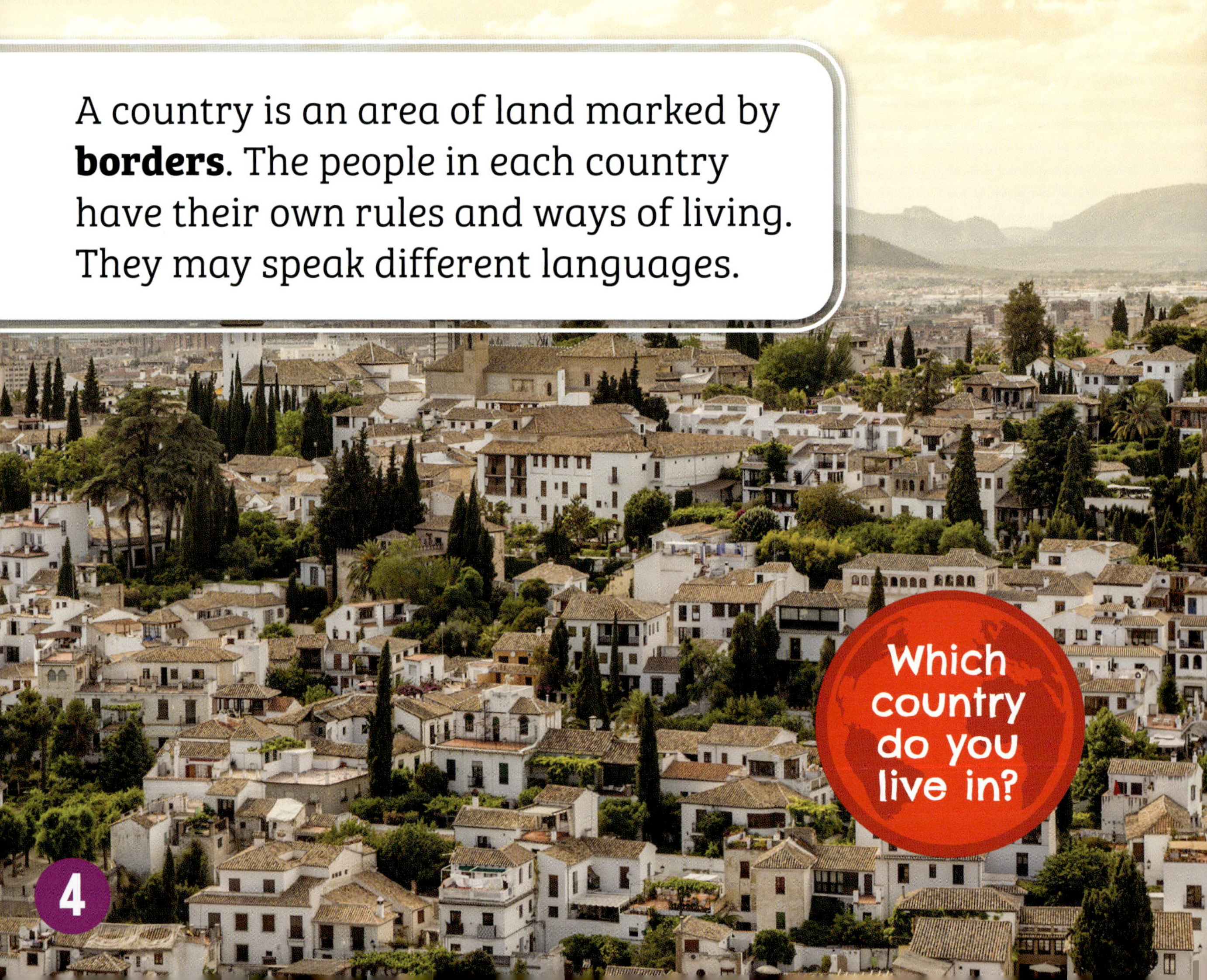

Which country do you live in?

Each country around the world has its own interesting things to see and do. Let's take a trip to visit a country and learn more!

Have you ever visited another country?

TODAY'S TRIP IS TO

SPAIN!

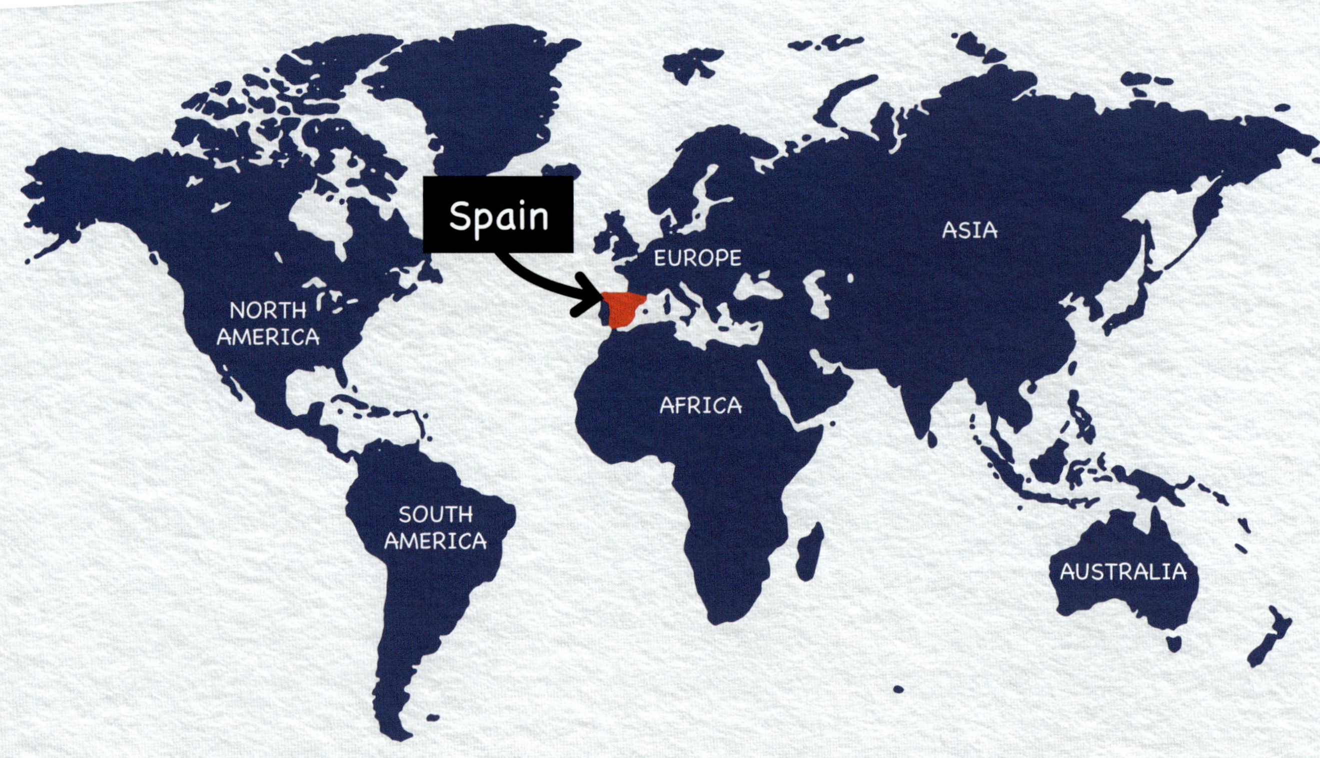

Spain is a country in the **continent** of Europe.

FACT FILE

Capital city: Madrid
Main language: Spanish
Currency: Euro
Flag:

Currency is the type of money that is used in a country.

MADRID

We'll start our trip in Spain's capital city, Madrid! It has lots of beautiful parks and famous museums.

Madrid is also where we'll find Palacio Real de Madrid. This palace has been home to the Spanish royal family for hundreds of years. It is the largest royal palace in Western Europe.

ART, MUSIC, AND DANCE

Art is an important part of Spanish **culture**. The country has been home to famous artists, including Pablo Picasso and Salvador Dalí. The work of these artists and others can be seen at Spain's many art museums.

Several kinds of music and dancing have come from Spain, too. The most famous of these is flamenco. It is a lively style of dance and music with guitar, **castanets**, and clapping.

FESTIVALS

Ready for some fun? Spain has hundreds of **festivals**. La Tomatina festival gets a little messy. Thousands of people from all over the world travel to the little town of Buñol for a big tomato fight in the streets!

A festival in the city of Grenada brings together some of the world's best musicians and dancers. They perform all around Granada, turning the whole city into a stage.

FOOD

All the **ingredients** for *paella* are mixed together in one pan.

Time to eat! *Paella* is a yummy food from a part of Spain called Valencia. This dish is made from rice, saffron, meat, and vegetables.

Spain is also known for *tortilla Española*. This delicious dish is made of egg, potato, and onion.

SAGRADA FAMÍLIA

Next, let's go to the city of Barcelona, where we'll find the Sagrada Família **temple**. This building was designed by Antoni Gaudí, who is considered one of Spain's best **architects**.

People started building the temple in 1882 and have been working on it ever since. Although it is not finished, Sagrada Família is still used for **worship**. The temple has church services in many languages for people visiting.

ANIMALS

Let's head into nature to see some animals! Spanish ibexes are wild goats that live on the steep, rocky slopes of mountains.

The Iberian lynx can also be found in Spain. This animal is among the most **endangered** wildcats in the world. Iberian lynxes have big ears, a short tail, and long legs.

SPANISH ISLANDS

There are more than 60 Spanish islands.

Most of Spain's land is between the countries of France and Portugal. However, Spain also has many islands in the Atlantic Ocean and the Mediterranean Sea.

Some of the islands, such as the Balearic and Canary Islands, are popular vacation spots. Other islands are too small to have **docks** for boats or airports for planes.

BEFORE YOU GO

We can't forget to see the Temple of Debod! The country of Egypt gave this **ancient** temple to Spain. To move it, people had to take apart the temple and then put it back together.

The temple sits in the Parque del Oeste in Madrid. If we walk around the rest of this park, we'll see impressive statues and a pretty rose garden, too.

Glossary

ancient from a long time ago

architects people who design buildings

borders lines that show where one place ends and another begins

castanets a musical instrument made of two parts that people click together with their fingers

continent one of the world's seven large land masses

culture the beliefs and ways of life shared by a group of people

docks places along coasts where boats can stop

endangered having become very rare and at risk of dying out completely

festivals events for lots of people to come together and celebrate

ingredients things used to make food

temple a building where people go to pray or worship

worship to honor or respect someone or something as a god

Index